ALSO BY CHARLES WRIGHT

POETRY

The Grave of the Right Hand (1970)
Hard Freight (1973)
Bloodlines (1975)
China Trace (1977)

TRANSLATIONS

The Storm and Other Things by Eugenio Montale (1978)

THE
SOUTHERN
CROSS

RANDOM HOUSE NEW YORK

THE
SOUTHERN
CROSS

CHARLES
WRIGHT

The first two sections were previously published in a small-press edition by Grilled Flowers Press, entitled *Wright: A Profile*.

Parts of Section III were published in a limited fine-press edition entitled *Dead Color* by The Meadow Press, San Francisco, for Charles Seluzicki, Fine Books, Salem, Oregon.

"Self-Portrait #3," "Holy Thursday," "Virginia Reel," and "Ars Poetica" originally appeared in *Antaeus*.

"Homage to Paul Cézanne," "October," "California Spring," "Laguna Dantesca," "Hawaii Dantesca," "Bar Giamica," and "Dog Day Vespers" originally appeared in *The New Yorker*.

Other selections first appeared in the following publications: *Crazy Horse, Durak, Field, The Iowa Review, Ironwood, The Missouri Review, New England Review, The Paris Review, Poetry Northwest, Quarterly West, Raccoon, The Seneca Review, Shenandoah,* and *Water Table*.

Grateful acknowledgment is also made to the Ingram Merrill Foundation for a grant which helped immensely toward the completion of this book.

Library of Congress Cataloging in Publication Data

Wright, Charles, 1935-
The Southern Cross.
Poems.
I. Title.
PS3573.R52S6   811'.54   81-40226
ISBN 0-394-52148-X   AACR 2
ISBN 0-394-74888-3 (pbk.)

FOR H.W. WILKINSON

Già s'inchinava ad abbracciar li piedi
  al mio dottor, ma el li disse: "Frate,
  non far, ché tu se' ombra e ombra vedi."
Ed ei surgendo: "Or puoi la quantitate
  comprender de l'amor ch'a te mi scalda,
  quand'io dismento nostra vanitate,
trattando l'ombre come cosa salda."
          —Dante, *Purgatorio,* XXI, 130–36

CONTENTS

I

II

III

IV

PART
ONE

HOMAGE TO PAUL CÉZANNE

At night, in the fish-light of the moon, the dead wear our white
  shirts
To stay warm, and litter the fields.
We pick them up in the mornings, dewy pieces of paper and
  scraps of cloth.
Like us, they refract themselves. Like us,
They keep on saying the same thing, trying to get it right.
Like us, the water unsettles their names.

Sometimes they lie like leaves in their little arks, and curl up at the
  edges.
Sometimes they come inside, wearing our shoes, and walk
From mirror to mirror.
Or lie in our beds with their gloves off
And touch our bodies. Or talk
In a corner. Or wait like envelopes on a desk.

They reach up from the ice plant.
They shuttle their messengers through the oat grass.
Their answers rise like rust on the stalks and the spidery leaves.

We rub them off our hands.

Each year the dead grow less dead, and nudge
Close to the surface of all things.
They start to remember the silence that brought them there.
They start to recount the gain in their soiled hands.

Their glasses let loose, and grain by grain return to the river bank.
They point to their favorite words
Growing around them, revealed as themselves for the first time:
They stand close to the meanings and take them in.

They stand there, vague and without pain,
Under their fingernails an unreturnable dirt.
They stand there and it comes back,
The music of everything, syllable after syllable

Out of the burning chair, out of the beings of light.
It all comes back.
And what they repeat to themselves, and what they repeat to
    themselves,
Is the song that our fathers sing.

In steeps and sighs,
The ocean explains itself, backing and filling
What spaces it can't avoid, spaces
In black shoes, their hands clasped, their eyes teared at the edges:
We watch from the high hillside,
The ocean swelling and flattening, the spaces
Filling and emptying, horizon blade
Flashing the early afternoon sun.

The dead are constant in
The white lips of the sea.
Over and over, through clenched teeth, they tell
Their story, the story each knows by heart:
Remember me, speak my name.
When the moon tugs at my sleeve,
When the body of water is raised and becomes the body of light,
Remember me, speak my name.

The dead are a cadmium blue.
We spread them with palette knives in broad blocks and planes.

We layer them stroke by stroke
In steps and ascending mass, in verticals raised from the earth.

We choose, and layer them in,
Blue and a blue and a breath,

Circle and smudge, cross-beak and buttonhook,
We layer them in. We squint hard and terrace them line by line.

And so we are come between, and cry out,
And stare up at the sky and its cloudy panes,

And finger the cypress twists.
The dead understand all this, and keep in touch,

Rustle of hand to hand in the lemon trees,
Flags, and the great sifts of anger

To powder and nothingness.
The dead are a cadmium blue, and they understand.

The dead are with us to stay.
Their shadows rock in the back yard, so pure, so black,
Between the oak tree and the porch.

Over our heads they're huge in the night sky.
In the tall grass they turn with the zodiac.
Under our feet they're white with the snows of a thousand years.

They carry their colored threads and baskets of silk
To mend our clothes, making us look right,
Altering, stitching, replacing a button, closing a tear.
They lie like tucks in our loose sleeves, they hold us together.

They blow the last leaves away.
They slide like an overflow into the river of heaven.
Everywhere they are flying.

The dead are a sleight and a fade
We fall for, like flowering plums, like white coins from the rain.
Their sighs are gaps in the wind.

The dead are waiting for us in our rooms,
Little globules of light
In one of the far corners, and close to the ceiling, hovering, think-
ing our thoughts.

Often they'll reach a hand down,
Or offer a word, and ease us out of our bodies to join them in
theirs.
We look back at our other selves on the bed.

We look back and we don't care and we go.

And thus we become what we've longed for,
                                        past tense and otherwise,
A BB, a disc of light,
                    song without words.
And refer to ourselves
In the third person, seeing that other arm
Still raised from the bed, fingers like licks and flames in the boned
air.

Only to hear that it's not time.
Only to hear that we must re-enter and lie still, our arms at rest
at our sides,
The voices rising around us like mist

And dew, *it's all right, it's all right, it's all right* . . .

The dead fall around us like rain.
They come down from the last clouds in the late light for the last
    time
And slip through the sod.

They lean uphill and face north.
                              Like grass,
They bend toward the sea, they break toward the setting sun.

We filigree and we baste.
But what do the dead care for the fringe of words,
Safe in their suits of milk?
What do they care for the honk and flash of a new style?

And who is to say if the inch of snow in our hearts
Is rectitude enough?

Spring picks the locks of the wind.
High in the night sky the mirror is hauled up and unsheeted.
In it we twist like stars.

Ahead of us, through the dark, the dead
Are beating their drums and stirring the yellow leaves.

We're out here, our feet in the soil, our heads craned up at the sky,
The stars streaming and bursting behind the trees.

At dawn, as the clouds gather, we watch
The mountain glide from the east on the valley floor,
Coming together in starts and jumps.
Behind their curtain, the bears
Amble across the heavens, serene as black coffee . . .

Whose unction can intercede for the dead?
Whose tongue is toothless enough to speak their piece?

What we are given in dreams we write as blue paint,
Or messages to the clouds.
At evening we wait for the rain to fall and the sky to clear.
Our words are words for the clay, uttered in undertones,
Our gestures salve for the wind.

We sit out on the earth and stretch our limbs,
Hoarding the little mounds of sorrow laid up in our hearts.

PART

TWO

SELF-PORTRAIT

Someday they'll find me out, and my lavish hands,
Full moon at my back, fog groping the gone horizon, the edge
Of the continent scored in yellow, expectant lights,
White shoulders of surf, a wolf-colored sand,
The ashes and bits of char that will clear my name.

Till then, I'll hum to myself and settle the whereabouts.
Jade plants and oleander float in a shine.
The leaves of the pepper tree turn green.
My features are sketched with black ink in a slow drag through
    the sky,
Waiting to be filled in.

Hand that lifted me once, lift me again,
Sort me and flesh me out, fix my eyes.
From the mulch and the undergrowth, protect me and pass me on.
From my own words and my certainties,
From the rose and the easy cheek, deliver me, pass me on.

MOUNT CARIBOU AT NIGHT

Just north of the Yaak River, one man sits bolt upright,
A little bonnet of dirt and bunch grass above his head:
Northwestern Montana is hard relief,
And harder still the lying down and the rising up . . .

I speak to the others there, lodged in their stone wedges, the blocks
And slashes that vein the ground, and tell them that Walter
    Smoot,
Starched and at ease in his bony duds
Under the tamaracks, still holds the nightfall between his knees.

Work stars, drop by inveterate drop, begin
Cassiopeia's sails and electric paste
Across the sky. And down
Toward the cadmium waters that carry them back to the dawn,

They squeeze out Andromeda and the Whale,
Everything on the move, everything flowing and folding back
And starting again,
Star-slick, the flaking and crusting duff at my feet,

Smoot and Runyan and August Binder
Still in the black pulse of the earth, cloud-gouache
Over the tree line, Mount Caribou
Massive and on the rise and taking it in. And taking it back

To the future we occupied, and will wake to again, ourselves
And our children's children snug in our monk's robes,
Pushing the cauly hoods back, ready to walk out
Into the same night and the meadow grass, in step and on time.

SELF-PORTRAIT

Charles on the Trevisan, night bridge
To the crystal, infinite alphabet of his past.
Charles on the San Trovaso, earmarked,
Holding the pages of a thrown-away book, dinghy the color of
   honey
Under the pine boughs, the water east-flowing.

The wind will edit him soon enough,
And squander his broken chords

                     in tiny striations above the air,
No slatch in the undertow.
The sunlight will bear him out,
Giving him breathing room, and a place to lie.

And why not? The reindeer still file through the bronchial trees,
Holding their heads high.
The mosses still turn, the broomstraws flash on and off.
Inside, in the crosslight, and St. Jerome
And his creatures . . . St. Augustine, striking the words out.

HOLY THURSDAY

Begins with the *ooo ooo* of a mourning dove
In the pepper tree, crack
Of blue and a flayed light on the hills,
Myself past the pumpkin blooms and out in the disked field,
Blake's children still hunched in sleep, dollops
Of bad dreams and an afterlife.
Canticles rise in spate from the bleeding heart.
Cathedrals assemble and disappear in the water beads.
I scuff at the slick adobe, one eye
On the stalk and one on the aftermath.

There's always a time for rust,
For looking down at the earth and its lateral chains.
There's always a time for the grass, teeming
Its little four-cornered purple flowers,
                              tricked out in an oozy shine.
There's always a time for the dirt.
Reprieve, reprieve, the flies drone, their wings
Increasingly incandescent above the corn silk.
No answer from anything, four crows
On a eucalyptus limb, speaking in tongues.
No answer for them, either.

It's noon in the medlar tree, the sun
Sifting its glitter across the powdery stems.
It doesn't believe in God
And still is absolved.
It doesn't believe in God

And seems to get by, going from here to there.
Butterflies blow like pieces of half-burned construction paper over
    the sweet weeds,
And take what is given them.
Some hummer is luckier
Downwind, and smells blood, and seeks me out.

The afternoon hangs by a leaf.
The vines are a green complaint
From the slaking adobe dust. I settle and stand back.
The hawk realigns herself.
Splatter of mockingbird notes, a brief trill from the jay.
The fog starts in, breaking its various tufts loose.
Everything smudges and glows,
Cactus, the mustard plants and the corn,
Through the white reaches of 4 o'clock . . .
There's always a time for words.

Surf sounds in the palm tree,
Susurrations, the wind
                    making a big move from the west,
The children asleep again, their second selves
Beginning to stir, the moon
Lop-sided, sliding their ladder down.
From under the billowing dead, from their wet hands and a saving
    grace,
The children begin to move, an angle of phosphorescence
Along the ridge line.

Angels
Are counting cadence, their skeletal songs
What the hymns say, the first page and the last.

SELF-PORTRAIT

The pictures in the air have few visitors.

Sun drops past tie-post in the east shallows,
Moon rises to camera range. Over the zodiac,
The numbers and definitions arc,
Hiwassee at low tide, my brother one step up the cleared slope.

Winter on top of the Matterhorn,
Sun-goggled, standing the way our father stood, hands half in his
    pockets.
Behind him, the summer Alps
Fall down and away, little hillocks of white on the noon sky
Hiding their crosses, keeping the story straight.

Like Munch, I languish, my left cheek in my left palm,
Omniscient above the bay,
Checking the evidence, the postcards and the photographs,
O'Grady's finger pointing me out . . .

Madonna of Tenderness, Lady of Feints and Xs, you point too.

VIRGINIA REEL

In Clarke County, the story goes, the family name
Was saved by a single crop of wheat,
The houses and land kept in a clear receipt for the subsequent
   suicides,
The hard times and non-believers to qualify and disperse:
Woodburn and Cedar Hall, Smithfield, Auburn and North Hill:
Names like white moths kicked up from the tall grass,
Spreading across the countryside
From the Shenandoah to Charles Town and the Blue Ridge.

And so it happened. But none of us lives here now, in any of them,
Though Aunt Roberta is still in town,
Close to the place my great-great-grandfather taught Nelly Cus-
   tis's children once
Answers to Luther. And Cardinal Newman too.
Who cares? Well, I do. It's worth my sighs
To walk here, on the wrong road, tracking a picture back
To its bricks and its point of view.
It's worth my while to be here, crumbling this dirt through my
   bare hands.

I've come back for the first time in 20 years,
Sand in my shoes, my pockets full of the same wind
That brought me before, my flesh
Remiss in the promises it made then, the absolutes it's heir to.
This is the road they drove on. And this is the rise
Their blood repaired to, removing its gloves.
And this is the dirt their lives were made of, the dirt the world is,
Immeasurable emptiness of all things.

I stand on the porch of Wickliffe Church,
My kinfolk out back in the bee-stitched vines and weeds,
The night coming on, my flat shirt drawing the light in,
Bright bud on the branch of nothing's tree.
In the new shadows, memory starts to shake out its dark cloth.
Everyone settles down, transparent and animate,
Under the oak trees.
Hampton passes the wine around, Jaq toasts to our health.

And when, from the blear and glittering air,
A hand touches my shoulder,
I want to fall to my knees, and keep on falling, here,
Laid down by the articles that bear my names,
The limestone and marble and locust wood.
But that's for another life. Just down the road, at Smithfield, the
    last of the apple blossoms
Fishtails to earth through the shot twilight,
A little vowel for the future, a signal from us to them.

SELF-PORTRAIT

Marostica, Val di Ser. Bassano del Grappa.
Madonna del Ortolo. San Giorgio, arc and stone.
The foothills above the Piave.

Places and things that caught my eye, Walt,
In Italy. On foot, Great Cataloguer, some 20-odd years ago.

San Zeno and Caffè Dante. Catullus' seat.
Lake Garda. The Adige at Ponte Pietra
—I still walk there, a shimmer across the bridge on hot days,
The dust, for a little while, lying lightly along my sleeve—.
Piazza Erbe, the 12 Apostles . . .

Over the grave of John Keats
The winter night comes down, her black habit starless and edged
    with ice,
Pure breaths of those who are rising from the dead.

Dino Campana, Arthur Rimbaud.
Hart Crane and Emily Dickinson. The Black Chateau.

CALLED BACK

Friday arrives with all its attendant ecstasies.
Mirrors bloom in the hushed beds.

The ocotillo starts to extend
                              its orange tongues
Down in Sonora, the cactus puts on its beads.
Juan Quesada's Angel of Death, socket and marrow bone,
Stares from its cage and scorched eyes.

I've made my overtures to the Black Dog, and backed off.
I've touched the links in its gold chain.
I've called out and bent down and even acknowledged my own
    face.

Darkness, O Father of Charity, lay on your hands.

For over an hour the joy of the mockingbird has altered the leaves.
Stealthily, blossoms have settled along the bougainvillaea like pur-
    ple moths
Catching their breaths, the sky still warm to the touch.
Nothing descends like snow or stiff wings
Out of the night.
                   Only the dew falls, soft as the footsteps of the dead.

Language can do just so much,
                              a flurry of prayers,
A chatter of glass beside the road's edge,
Flash and a half-glint as the headlights pass . . .

When the oak tree and the Easter grass have taken my body,
I'll start to count out my days, beginning at 1.

SELF-PORTRAIT

In Murray, Kentucky I lay once
On my side, the ghost-weight of a past life in my arms,
A life not mine. I know she was there,
Asking for nothing, heavy as bad luck, still waiting to rise.
I know now and I lift her.

Evening becomes us.
I see myself in a tight dissolve, and answer to no one.
Self-traitor, I smuggle in
The spider love, undoer and rearranger of all things.
Angel of Mercy, strip me down.

This world is a little place,
Just red in the sky before the sun rises.
Hold hands, hold hands
That when the birds start, none of us is missing.
Hold hands, hold hands.

PART
THREE

COMPOSITION IN GREY AND PINK

The souls of the day's dead fly up like birds, big sister,
The sky shutters and casts loose.
And faster than stars the body goes to the earth.

Heat hangs like a mist from the trees.
Butterflies pump through the banked fires of late afternoon.
The rose continues its sure rise to the self.

Ashes, trampled garlands . . .

I dream of an incandescent space
                              where nothing distinct exists,
And where nothing ends, the days sliding like warm milk through
   the clouds,
Everyone's name in chalk letters once and for all,

The dogstar descending with its pestilent breath . . .

Fatherless, stiller than still water,
I want to complete my flesh
                              and sit in a quiet corner
Untied from God, where the dead don't sing in their sleep.

LAGUNA BLUES

It's Saturday afternoon at the edge of the world.
White pages lift in the wind and fall.
Dust threads, cut loose from the heart, float up and fall.
Something's off-key in my mind.
Whatever it is, it bothers me all the time.

It's hot, and the wind blows on what I have had to say.
I'm dancing a little dance.
The crows pick up a thermal that angles away from the sea.
I'm singing a little song.
Whatever it is, it bothers me all the time.

It's Saturday afternoon and the crows glide down,
Black pages that lift and fall.
The castor beans and the pepper plant trundle their weary heads.
Something's off-key and unkind.
Whatever it is, it bothers me all the time.

OCTOBER

The leaves fall from my fingers.
Cornflowers scatter across the field like stars,
                                        like smoke stars,
By the train tracks, the leaves in a drift

Under the slow clouds
                    and the nine steps to heaven,
The light falling in great sheets through the trees,
Sheets almost tangible.

The transfiguration will start like this, I think,
                                        breathless,
Quick blade through the trees,
Something with red colors falling away from my hands,

The air beginning to go cold . . .
                                And when it does
I'll rise from this tired body, a blood-knot of light,
Ready to take the darkness in.

—Or for the wind to come
And carry me, bone by bone, through the sky,
Its wafer a burn on my tongue,
                                its wine deep forgetfulness.

CHILDHOOD'S BODY

This is a rope of stars tied to my wrist.
This is a train, pulling the feckless palmprints of the dead.

It isn't enough to sing and begin again.
It isn't enough to dissemble the alphabet

And listen for
The one heartbeat I listen for,
                          as it comes as it goes,
Keeping the world alive,

My poems in a language now
                          I finally understand,
Little tablets of salt rubbed smooth by the wind.

It isn't enough to transform the curlicues.

(Deep water is what the albums will manifest,
                          the light jagged then not jagged,
The moon dragging her hooks
Through the lakes and the river beds . . .)

This is a lip of snow and a lip of blood.

DRIVING THROUGH TENNESSEE

It's strange what the past brings back.
Our parents, for instance, how ardently they still loom
In the brief and flushed
Fleshtones of memory, one foot in front of the next
Even in retrospect, and so unimpeachable.

And towns that we lived in once,
And who we were then, the roads we went back and forth on
Returning ahead of us like rime
In the moonlight's fall, and Jesus returning, and Stephen Martyr
And St. Paul of the Sword . . .

—I am their music,
Mothers and fathers and places we hurried through in the night:
I put my mouth to the dust and sing their song.
Remember us, Galeoto, and whistle our tune, when the time
   comes,
For charity's sake.

SPRING ABSTRACT

The notes I fall for fall from the lip of the sky,
A thousand years of music unstrung by the wind.
What do I care for the noun and its adjective?
What do I care for the quick shimmer that comes
Like a burning line so quietly toward me across the lake?

The green gloves of the fig tree unfold in the sun.
Jonquils slit from their shells.
And the bees plunder, glistening in and out
As they drag the Queens of the Night and the lime blossoms,
Rubbing the sleep from their eyes . . .

The hair of the full moon is pulled back.
The shrink of the warmed dew breaks off on the blades,
One line in the page that heaven and earth make.
Meager and rumpled, wrung out,
The poem is ground down from a mumbled joy.

LANDSCAPE WITH SEATED
FIGURE AND OLIVE TREES

Orange blossoms have dropped their threads
On the stone floor of the heart
                              more often than once
Between last night's stars and last night's stars.
And the Preludes have left their rings
On the chalk white of the walls.
                    And the slide-harp has played and played.

And now, under the fruit trees,
                        the olives silver then not silver, the wind
In them then not, the old man
Sits in the sunfall,
Slouched and at ease in the sunfall, the leaves tipped in the wind.

The world is nothing to him.
And the music is nothing to him, and the noon sun.
Only the wind matters.
Only the wind as it moves through the tin shine of the leaves.
And the orange blossoms,
          scattered like poems on the smooth stones.

DOG YOGA

A spring day in the weeds.
A thread of spittle across the sky, and a thread of ash.
Mournful cadences from the clouds.

Through the drives and the cypress beds,
                                        25 years of sad news.

Mother of Thrushes, Our Lady of Crows,
Brief as a handkerchief,
                                25 years of sad news.

Later, stars and sea winds in and out of the open window.

Later, and lonesome among the sleepers,
                                the day's thunder in hidden places,
One lissome cheek a notch in the noontide's leash,

A ghostly rain of sunlight among the ferns.

Year in, year out, the same loom from the dark.
Year in, year out, the same sound in the wind.

Near dawn, the void in the heart,
The last coat of lacquer along the leaves,
                                the quench in the west.

CALIFORNIA SPRING

                                             .

At dawn the dove croons.
A hawk hangs over the field.
The liquidambar rinses its hundred hands.

And the light comes on in the pepper trees.
Under its flat surfaces horns and noises are starting up.
The dew drops begin to shrink.

How sad the morning is.
There is a tree which rains down in the field.
There is a spider that swings back and forth on his thin strings in
    the heart.

How cold the wind is.
And the sun is, caught like a kite in the drooped limbs of the tree.
The apricot blossoms scatter across the ice plant.

One angel dangles his wing.
The grass edges creak and the tide pools begin to shine.
Nothing forgives.

LAGUNA DANTESCA

I want, like a little boat, to be isolate,
                              slipping across one element
Toward the horizon, whose lips know something but stay sealed
                    under the heaven of the moon.

There's something I want to look on, face to face.

Like a rock, or some other heavy thing, I want to descend through
    clear water
Endlessly,
              disappearing as she did,
Line after leached line, into the lunar deeps.

I want, like these lavender bells from the jacaranda tree,
To flare with the fixed stars,
                              used up and self-satisfied.

Tree frogs drum in the dark. The small brass of the natural world
Is drumming and what I want
                              is nothing to them.

Above me, the big dog lies low in the southern sky and bides its
    time.

Like a scrap of charred paper, I want to return.
There's something I want to look on whose face
                              rises and falls like a flame.

I want to sit down there, the dog asleep at my feet.

DOG DAY VESPERS

Sun like an orange mousse through the trees,
A snowfall of trumpet bells on the oleander;

                                    mantis paws
Craning out of the new wisteria; fruit smears in the west . . .
DeStael knifes a sail on the bay;
A mother's summons hangs like a towel on the dusk's hook.

Everything drips and spins
In the pepper trees, the pastel glide of the evening
Slowing to mother-of-pearl and the night sky.
Venus breaks clear in the third heaven.
Quickly the world is capped, and the seal turned.

I drag my chair to the deck's edge and the blue ferns.
I'm writing you now by flashlight,
The same news and the same story I've told you often before.
As the stag-stars begin to shine,
A wing brushes my left hand,

                                    but it's not my wing.

PORTRAIT OF THE ARTIST
WITH HART CRANE

It's Venice, late August, outside after lunch, and Hart
Is stubbing his cigarette butt in a wine glass,
The look on his face pre-moistened and antiseptic,
A little like death or a smooth cloud.
The watery light of his future still clings in the pergola.

The subject of all poems is the clock,
I think, those tiny, untouchable hands that fold across our chests
Each night and unfold each morning, finger by finger
Under the new weight of the sun.
One day more is one day less.

I've been writing this poem for weeks now
With a pencil made of rain, smudging my face
And my friend's face, making a language where nothing stays.
The sunlight has no such desire.
In the small pools of our words, its business is radiance.

PORTRAIT OF THE ARTIST
WITH LI PO

The "high heavenly priest of the White Lake" is now
A small mound in an endless plain of grass,
His pendants clicking and pearls shading his eyes.
He never said anything about the life after death,
Whose body is clothed in a blue rust and the smoke of dew.

He liked flowers and water most.
Everyone knows the true story of how he would write his verses
    and float them,
Like paper boats, downstream
                        just to watch them drift away.
Death never entered his poems, but rowed, with its hair down, far
    out on the lake,
Laughing and looking up at the sky.

Over a 1000 years later, I write out one of his lines in a notebook,
The peach blossom follows the moving water,
And watch the October darkness gather against the hills.
All night long the river of heaven will move westward while no
    one notices.
The distance between the dead and the living
                  is more than a heart beat and a breath.

THE MONASTERY AT VRŠAC

We've walked the grounds,
                        inspected the vaults and the old church,
Looked at the icons and carved stalls,

And followed the path to the bishop's grave.

Now we sit in the brandy-colored light of late afternoon
Under the locust trees,
                    attended and small
From the monastery. Two nuns hop back and forth like grackles
Along the path. The light drips from the leaves.

Little signals of dust rise uninterpreted from the road.
The grass drones in its puddle of solitude.

The stillness is awful, as though from the inside of a root . . .

—Time's sluice and the summer rains erode our hearts
                        and carry our lives away.
We hold what we can in our two hands,
Sinking, each year, another inch in the earth . . .

Mercy upon us,
                we who have learned to preach but not to pray.

DEAD COLOR

I lie for a long time on my left side and my right side
And eat nothing,
                    but no voice comes on the wind
And no voice drops from the cloud.
Between the grey spiders and the orange spiders,
                              no voice comes on the wind . . .

Later, I sit for a long time by the waters of Har,
And no face appears on the face of the deep.

Meanwhile, the heavens assemble their dark map.
The traffic begins to thin.
Aphids munch on the sweet meat of the lemon trees.
The lawn sprinklers rise and fall . . .

And here's a line of brown ants cleaning a possum's skull.
And here's another, come from the opposite side.

Over my head, star-pieces dip in their yellow scarves toward their
    black desire.

Windows, rapturous windows!

HAWAII DANTESCA

White-sided flowers are thrusting up on the hillside,
                              blank love letters from the dead.
It's autumn, and nobody seems to mind.

Or the broken shadows of those missing for hundreds of years
Moving over the sugar cane
                              like storks, which nobody marks or mends.

This is the story line.

And the viridescent shirtwaists of light the trees wear.
And the sutra-circles of cattle egrets wheeling out past the rain
    showers.
And the spiked marimbas of dawn rattling their amulets . . .

Soon it will be time for the long walk under the earth toward the
    sea.

And time to retrieve the yellow sunsuit and little shoes
                              they took my picture in
In Knoxville, in 1938.

Time to gather the fire in its quartz bowl.

I hope the one with the white wings will come.
I hope the island of reeds is as far away as I think it is.

When I get there, I hope they forgive me if the knot I tie is the
    wrong knot.

ARS POETICA

I like it back here

Under the green swatch of the pepper tree and the aloe vera.
I like it because the wind strips down the leaves without a word.
I like it because the wind repeats itself,

and the leaves do.

I like it because I'm better here than I am there,

Surrounded by fetishes and figures of speech:
Dog's tooth and whale's tooth, my father's shoe, the dead weight
Of winter, the inarticulation of joy . . .

The spirits are everywhere.

And once I have them called down from the sky, and spinning and
dancing in the palm of my hand,
What will it satisfy?

I'll still have

The voices rising out of the ground,
The fallen star my blood feeds,

this business I waste my heart on.

And nothing stops that.

BAR GIAMAICA, 1959–60

Grace is the focal point,
                              the tip ends of her loosed hair
Like match fire in the back light,
Her hands in a "Here's the church . . . "
                                        She's looking at Ugo Mulas,
Who's looking at us.

Ingrid is writing this all down, and glances up, and stares hard.

This still isn't clear.

I'm looking at Grace, and Goldstein and Borsuk and Dick Venezia
Are looking at me.
                        Yola keeps reading her book.

And that leaves the rest of them: Susan and Elena and Carl Glass.
And Thorp and Schimmel and Jim Gates,
                                        and Hobart and Schneeman

One afternoon in Milan in the late spring.

Then Ugo finishes, drinks a coffee, and everyone goes away.
Summer arrives, and winter;
                              the snow falls and no one comes back
Ever again,
              all of them gone through the star filter of memory,
With its small gravel and metal tables and passers-by . . .

GATE CITY BREAKDOWN

Like a vein of hard coal, it was the strike
We fantasized, the pocket of sure reward we sidestepped the
   roadblocks for
In Southwest Virginia, seamed in its hillside
Above the north fork of the Holston River.

One afternoon before Christmas
In 1953, we crossed the bridge from Tennessee on a whiskey run,
Churchill and Bevo Hammond and Philbeck and I,
All home for the holidays.
On the back road where they chased us, we left the Sheriff's Patrol
   in their own dust,
And washed ours down with Schlitz on the way home.

Jesus, it's so ridiculous, and full of self-love,
The way we remember ourselves,
                              and the dust we leave . . .

Remember me as you will, but remember me once
Slide-wheeling around the curves,
                        letting it out on the other side of the line.

NEW YEAR'S EVE, 1979

After the picture show, the explanation is usually found in
The moralistic overtones of our lives:
We are what we've always been,
Everybody uses somebody,
In the slow rise to the self, we're drawn up by many hands.

And so it is here.
                    Will Charles look on happiness in this life?
Will the past be the present ever again?
Will the dead abandon their burdens and walk to the river bank?

In this place, at year's end, under a fitful moon, tide pools
Spindle the light.
Across their floors, like spiders,
Hermit crabs quarter and spin.
                    Their sky is a glaze and a day . . .

What matters to them is what comes up from below, and from out
    there
In the deep water,
                    and where the deep water comes from.

Laguna Beach

PART
FOUR

The crocus blow in autumn.

THE SOUTHERN CROSS

Things that divine us we never touch:

The black sounds of the night music,
The Southern Cross, like a kite at the end of its string,

And now this sunrise, and empty sleeve of a day,
The rain just starting to fall, and then not fall,

No trace of a story line.

———————

All day I've remembered a lake and a sudsy shoreline,
Gauze curtains blowing in and out of open windows all over the
    South.

It's 1936, in Tennessee. I'm one
And spraying the dead grass with a hose.
The curtains blow in and out.

And then it's not. And I'm not and they're not.

Or it's 1941 in a brown suit, or '53 in its white shoes,
Overlay after overlay tumbled and brought back,
As meaningless as the sea would be
                    if the sea could remember its waves . . .

———————

Nothing had told me my days were marked for a doom
        under the cold stars of the Virgin.
Nothing had told me that woe would buzz at my side like a fly.

The morning is dark with spring.
The early blooms on the honeysuckle shine like maggots after the
 rain.
The purple mouths of the passion blossoms
        open their white gums to the wind.

How sweet the past is, no matter how wrong, or how sad.
How sweet is yesterday's noise.

       ————

All day the ocean was like regret,
      clearing its throat, brooding and self-absorbed.

Now the wisteria tendrils extend themselves like swan's necks
 under Orion.

Now the small stars in the orange trees.

       ————

At Garda, on Punto San Vigilio, the lake,
In springtime, is like the sea,
Wind fishtailing the olive leaves like slash minnows beneath the
 vineyards,

Ebb and flow of the sunset past Sirmio,
                              flat voice of the waters
Retelling their story, again and again, as though to unburden itself

Of an unforgotten guilt,
                              and not relieved
Under the soothing hand of the dark,

The clouds over Bardolino dragging the sky for the dead
Bodies of those who refuse to rise,
Their orange robes and flaming bodices trolling across the hills,

Nightwind by now in the olive trees,
No sound but the wind from anything
                              under the tired, Italian stars . . .

And the voice of the waters, starting its ghostly litany.

_____

River of sighs and forgetfulness
                              (and the secret light Campana saw),
River of bloom-bursts from the moon,
                              of slivers and broken blades from the moon
In an always-going-away of glints . . .

Dante and Can Grande once stood here,
Next to the cool breath of S. Anastasia,
                              watching the cypress candles
Flare in their deep green across the Adige
In the Giusti Gardens.

Before that, in his marble tier,
Catullus once sat through the afternoons.
Before that, God spoke in the rocks . . .

And now it's my turn to stand
Watching a different light do the same things on a different water,
The Adige bearing its gifts
                    through the April twilight of 1961.

———————

When my father went soldiering, apes dropped from the trees.
When my mother wrote home from bed, the stars asked for a
    pardon.

They're both ghosts now, haunting the chairs and the sugar chest.

From time to time I hear their voices drifting like smoke through
    the living room,
Touching the various things they owned once.
Now they own nothing
                    and drift like smoke through the living room.

———————

Thinking of Dante, I start to feel
What I think are wings beginning to push out from my shoulder
    blades,
And the firm pull of water under my feet.

52

Thinking of Dante, I think of La Pia,
                                    and Charles Martel
And Cacciaguida inside the great flower of Paradise,
And the thin stem of Purgatory
                              rooted in Hell.

Thinking of Dante is thinking about the other side,
And the other side of the other side.
It's thinking about the noon noise and the daily light.

———————

Here is the truth. The wind rose, the sea
Shuffled its blue deck and dealt you a hand:
Blank, blank, blank, blank, blank.
Pelicans rode on the flat back of the waves through the green
    afternoon.
Gulls malingered along its breezes.
The huge cross of an airplane's shadow hurried across the sand,
                                    but no one stayed on it
For long, and nobody said a word.
You could see the island out past the orange gauze of the smog.

———————

The Big Dipper has followed me all the days of my life.
Under its tin stars my past has come and gone.
Tonight, in the April glaze
                          and scrimshaw of the sky,

It blesses me once again
With its black water, and sends me on.

————

After 12 years it's hard to recall
That defining sound the canal made at sundown, slap
Of tide swill on the church steps,
Little runnels of boat wash slipping back from the granite slabs
In front of Toio's, undulant ripples
Flattening out in small hisses, the oily rainbows regaining their
    loose shapes
Silently, mewling and quick yelps of the gulls
Wheeling from shadow into the pink and grey light over the
    Zattere,
Lapping and rocking of water endlessly,
At last like a low drone in the dark shell of the ear
As the night lifted like mist from the Ogni Santi
And San Sebastiano
                        into the cold pearl of the sky . . .

All that year it lullabied just outside my window
As Venice rode through my sleep like a great spider,
Flawless and Byzantine,
                        webbed like glass in its clear zinc.
In winter the rain fell
                        and the locust fell.
In summer the sun rose
Like a whetstone over the steel prows of the gondolas,

Their silver beak-blades rising and falling,
                              the water whiter than stone.
In autumn the floods came, and oil as thick as leaves in the entry
    way.
In spring, at evening, under the still-warm umbrellas,
We watched the lights blaze and extend
                              along the rio,
And watched the black boats approaching, almost without sound.
And still the waters sang lullaby.

I remember myself as a figure among the colonnades,
Leaning from left to right,
                    one hand in my pocket,
The way the light fell,
                    the other one holding me up.
I remember myself as a slick on the slick canals,
Going the way the tide went,
The city sunk to her knees in her own reflection.
I remember the way that Pound walked
                              across San Marco
At *passeggiata,* as though with no one,
                              his eyes on the long ago.
I remember the time that Tate came.
                              And Palazzo Guggenheim
When the floods rose
                    and the boat took us all the way
Through the front doors and down to the back half
Of *da Montin,* where everyone was, clapping their hands.

What's hard to remember is how the wind moved and the reeds
  clicked
Behind Torcello,
              little bundles of wind in the marsh grass
Chasing their own tails, and skidding across the water.
What's hard to remember is how the electric lights
Were played back, and rose and fell on the black canal
Like swamp flowers,
                  shrinking and stretching,
Yellow and pale and iron-blue from the oil.
It's hard to remember the way the snow looked
                              on San Gregorio,
And melting inside the pitch tubs and the smoke of San Trovaso,
The gondolas beached and stripped,
The huge snowflakes planing down through the sea-heavy air
Like dead moths,
              drifting and turning . . .

_____

As always, silence will have the last word,
And Venice will lie like silk
              at the edge of the sea and the night sky,
Albescent under the moon.

Everyone's life is the same life
                      if you live long enough.

_____

Orioles shuttle like gold thread
                    through the grey cloth of daylight.
The fog is so low and weighted down
Crows fall through like black notes from the sky.
The orioles stitch and weave.
Somewhere below, the ocean nervously grinds its teeth
As the morning begins to take hold
                            and the palm trees gleam.

─────────

There is an otherness inside us
We never touch,
                    no matter how far down our hands reach.
It is the past,
            with its good looks and *Anytime, Anywhere* . . .
Our prayers go out to it, our arms go out to it
Year after year,
But who can ever remember enough?

─────────

Friday again, with its sack of bad dreams
And long-legged birds,
                    a handful of ashes for this and that
In the streets, and some for the squat piano.

Friday beneath the sky, its little postcards of melancholy
Outside each window,
                    the engines inside the roses at half speed,
The huge page of the sea with its one word *despair*,

Fuchsia blossoms littered across the deck,
Unblotted tide pools of darkness beneath the ferns . . .
And still I go on looking,

                match after match in the black air.

———————

The lime, electric green of the April sea

                off Ischia

Is just a thumb-rub on the window glass between here and there:
And the cloud cap above the volcano
That didn't move when the sea wind moved;
And the morning the doves came, low from the mountain's
    shadow,

                        under the sunlight,

Over the damp tops of the vine rows,
Eye-high in a scythe slip that dipped and rose and cut down
    toward the sea;
And the houses like candy wrappers blown up against the hillside
Above Sant'Angelo,

              fuchsia and mauve and cyclamen;

And the story Nicola told,
How the turtle doves come up from Africa
On the desert winds,

             how the hunters take the fresh seeds

From their crops and plant them,
The town windows all summer streaked with the nameless blooms.

The landscape was always the best part.

Places swim up and sink back, and days do,
The edges around what really happened
                              we'll never remember
No matter how hard we stare back at the past:

One April, in downtown Seville,
                              alone on an Easter morning
Wasted in emerald light from the lemon trees,
I watched a small frog go back and forth on the lily pads
For hours, and still don't know
                              just what I was staying away from . . .

(And who could forget Milano in '59,
                              all winter under the rain?
Cathedrals for sure,
And dry stops in the Brera,
                  all of her boulevards ending in vacant lots.

And Hydra and Mykonos,
Barely breaking the calm with their white backs
As they roll over
                  and flash back down to the dark . . .)

Places swim up and sink back, and days do,
Larger and less distinct each year,
As we are,
                  and lolling about in the same redress,
Leaves and insects drifting by on their windows.

Rome was never like that,
                    and the Tiber was never like that,
Nosing down from the Apennines,
                    color of *café-au-lait* as it went through town . . .

Still, I can't remember the name of one street
                                        near Regina Coeli,
Or one block of the Lungotevere on either side,
Or one name of one shop on Campo dei Fiori.
Only Giordano Bruno,
                    with his razed look and black caul,
Rises unbidden out of the blank
Unruffled waters of memory,
                              his martyred bronze
Gleaming and still wet in the single electric light.

I can't remember the colors I said I'd never forget
On Via Giulia at sundown,
The ochres and glazes and bright hennas of each house,
Or a single day from November of 1964.
I can't remember the way the stairs smelled
                                        or the hallway smelled
At Piazza del Biscione.
                        Or just how the light fell
Through the east-facing window over the wicker chairs there.

I do remember the way the boar hung
                        in the butcher shop at Christmas

Two streets from the Trevi fountain, a crown of holly and
   mistletoe
Jauntily over his left ear.
I do remember the flower paintings
Nodding throughout the May afternoons
                         on the dining room walls
At Zajac's place.
              And the reliquary mornings,
And Easter, and both Days of the Dead . . .

At noon in the English Cemetery no one's around.
Keats is off to the left, in an open view.
Shelley and Someone's son are straight up ahead.

With their marble breath and their marble names,
                  the sun in a quick squint through the trees,
They lie at the edge of everywhere,
               Rome like a stone cloud at the back of their eyes.

————

Time is the villain in most tales,
                and here, too,
Lowering its stiff body into the water.
Its landscape is the resurrection of the word,
No end of it,
            the petals of wreckage in everything.

————

I've been sitting here tracking the floor plan
                            of a tiny, mottled log spider
Across the front porch of the cabin,
And now she's under my chair,
                            off to her own devices,
Leaving me mine, and I start watching the two creeks

Come down through the great meadow
Under the lodgepole pine and the willow run,
The end of June beginning to come clear in the clouds,
Shadows like drowned men where the creeks go under the hill.

Last night, in the flood run of the moon, the bullbats
Diving out of the yellow sky
                            with their lonesome and jungly whistling,
I watched, as I've watched before, the waters send up their smoke
    signals of blue mist,
And thought, for the 1st time,
                I half-understood what they keep on trying to say.

But now I'm not sure.
                Behind my back, the spider has got her instructions
And carries them out.
Flies drone, wind back-combs the marsh grass, swallows bank and
    climb.
Everything I can see knows just what to do,

Even the dragonfly, hanging like lapis lazuli in the sun . . .

_____

I can't remember enough.

How the hills, for instance, at dawn in Kingsport
In late December in 1962 were black
                          against a sky
The color of pale fish blood and water that ran to white
As I got ready to leave home for the 100th time,
My mother and father asleep,
                          my sister asleep,
Carter's Valley as dark as the inside of a bone
Below the ridge,
                   the 1st knobs of the Great Smokies
Beginning to stick through the sunrise,
The hard pull of a semi making the grade up US 11W,
The cold with its metal teeth ticking against the window,
The long sigh of the screen door stop,
My headlights starting to disappear
                          in the day's new turning . . .

I'll never be able to.

—————

Sunday, a brute bumblebee working the clover tops
Next to the step I'm sitting on,
                          sticking his huge head
Into each tiny, white envelope.
The hot sun of July, in the high Montana air, bastes a sweet glaze
On the tamarack and meadow grass.

In the blue shadows
                    moist curls of the lupin glide
And the bog lilies extinguish their mellow lamps . . .

Sunday, a *Let us pray* from the wind, a glint
Of silver among the willows.
                              The lilacs begin to bleed
In their new sleep, and the golden vestments of morning
Lift for a moment, then settle back into place.
The last of the dog roses offers itself by the woodpile.
Everything has its work,
                         everything written down
In a second-hand grace of solitude and tall trees . . .

August licks at the pine trees.
Sun haze, and little fugues from the creek.
Fern-sleep beneath the green skirt of the marsh.

I always imagine a mouth
Starting to open its blue lips
Inside me, an arm
                   curving sorrowfully over an open window
At evening, and toads leaping out of the wet grass.

Again the silence of flowers.
Again the faint notes of piano music back in the woods.
How easily summer fills the room.

The life of this world is wind.
Wind-blown we come, and wind-blown we go away.
All that we look on is windfall.
All we remember is wind.

———

Pickwick was never the wind . . .

It's what we forget that defines us, and stays in the same place,
And waits to be rediscovered.
Somewhere in all that network of rivers and roads and silt hills,
A city I'll never remember,
                    its walls the color of pure light,
Lies in the August heat of 1935,
In Tennessee, the bottom land slowly becoming a lake.
It lies in a landscape that keeps my imprint
Forever,
            and stays unchanged, and waits to be filled back in.
Someday I'll find it out
And enter my old outline as though for the 1st time,

And lie down, and tell no one.

NOTES

Virginia Reel is for Mark Strand.

Landscape with Seated Figure and Olive Trees: Ezra Pound at Sant'Ambrogio.

Laguna Dantesca: "She" is Picarda Donati, *Paradiso,* III.

Dog Day Vespers is for David Young.

Hawaii Dantesca: Dante and the reed of humility, *Purgatorio,* I.

Bar Giamaica 1959–60: Ugo Mulas, Italian photographer, 1928–73.

The Southern Cross is for Mark Jarman.

ABOUT THE AUTHOR

CHARLES WRIGHT was born in Pickwick Dam, Tennessee, in 1935 and was educated at Davidson College and the University of Iowa. His books of poetry include *The Grave of the Right Hand* (1970), *Hard Freight* (1973), *Bloodlines* (1975), and *China Trace* (1977). *Hard Freight* was nominated for the National Book Award in poetry, and Mr. Wright's translation of the Italian poet Eugenio Montale's *The Storm and Other Things* won the 1978 P.E.N. Translation Prize.

Mr. Wright received the Edgar Allan Poe Award administered by the Academy of American Poets in 1976 and an Academy-Institute Grant from the American Academy and Institute of Arts and Letters in 1977. He teaches at the University of California at Irvine.